LETHAL STRIKERS

SOUTH AMERICA'S DEADLY RATTLESNAKE

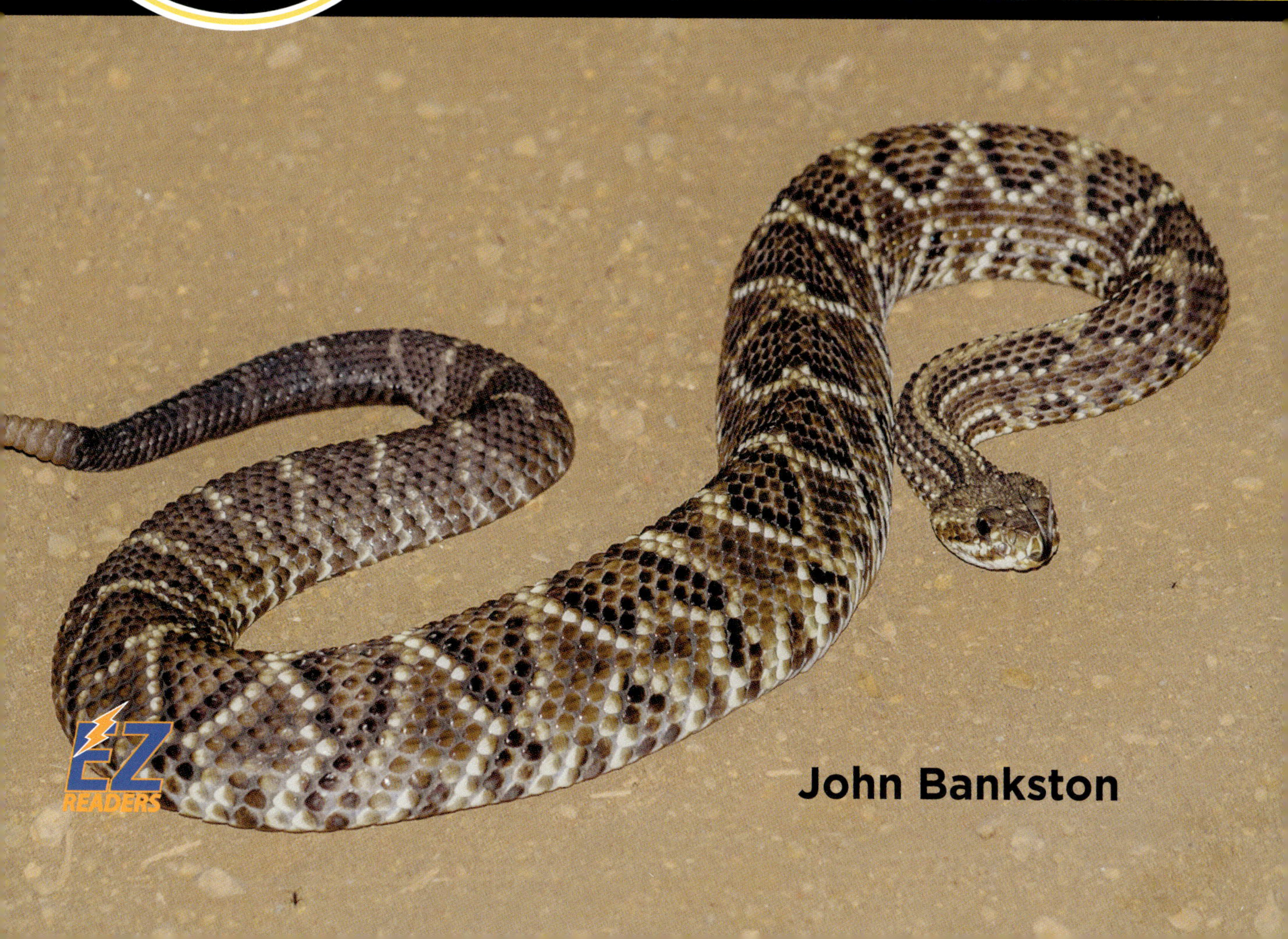

EZ READERS

John Bankston

Creating Young Nonfiction Readers

EZ Readers lets children delve into nonfiction at beginning reading levels. Young readers are introduced to new concepts, facts, ideas, and vocabulary.

Tips for Reading Nonfiction with Beginning Readers

Talk about Nonfiction
Begin by explaining that nonfiction books give us information that is true. The book will be organized around a specific topic or idea, and we may learn new facts through reading.

Look at the Parts
Most nonfiction books have helpful features. Our *EZ Readers* include a Contents page, an index, and color photographs. Share the purpose of these features with your reader.

Contents
Located at the front of a book, the Contents displays a list of the big ideas within the book and where to find them.

Index
An index is an alphabetical list of topics and the page numbers where they are found.

Photos/Charts
A lot of information can be found by "reading" the charts and photos found within nonfiction text. Help your reader learn more about the different ways information can be displayed.

With a little help and guidance about reading nonfiction, you can feel good about introducing a young reader to the world of *EZ Readers* nonfiction books.

Mitchell Lane
PUBLISHERS

2001 SW 31st Avenue
Hallandale, FL 33009
www.mitchelllane.com

First Edition, 2023.

Author: John Bankston
Designer: Ed Morgan
Editor: Morgan Brody

Title: South America's Deadly Rattlesnake
Description: Hallandale, FL : Mitchell Lane Publishers, [2023]

Series: Lethal Strikers: Latin America's Deadliest Snakes
Library bound ISBN: 978-1-68020-789-7
eBook ISBN: 978-1-68020-790-3

EZ Readers is an imprint of Mitchell Lane Publishers.

Photo credits: Shutterstock

CONTENTS

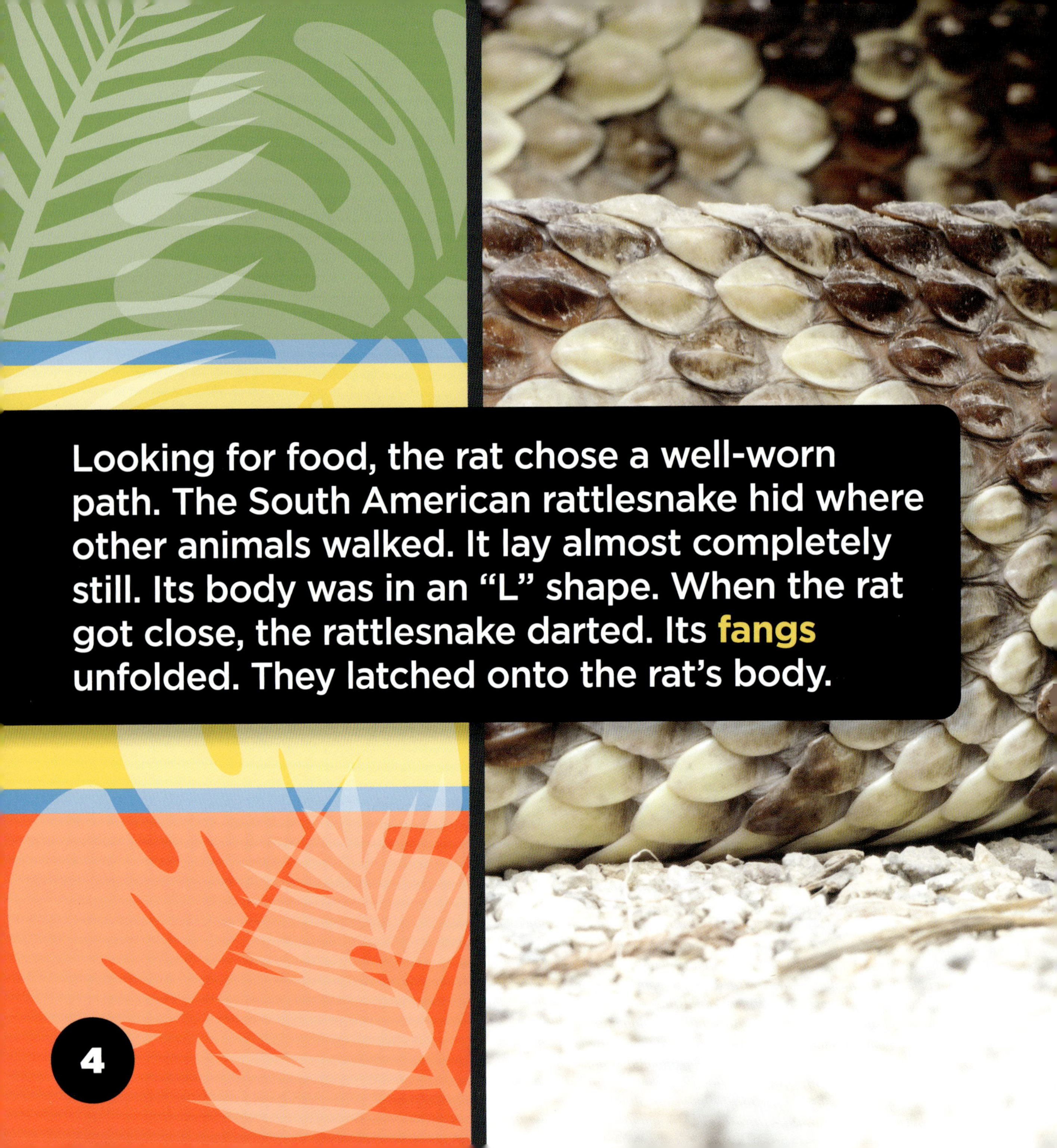

Looking for food, the rat chose a well-worn path. The South American rattlesnake hid where other animals walked. It lay almost completely still. Its body was in an "L" shape. When the rat got close, the rattlesnake darted. Its **fangs** unfolded. They latched onto the rat's body.

Powerful **venom** slowed the rat's heart. The snake let the rat go. It tickled the rat with its tongue to make sure it was dead. Then the snake opened its mouth and swallowed the rat head first.

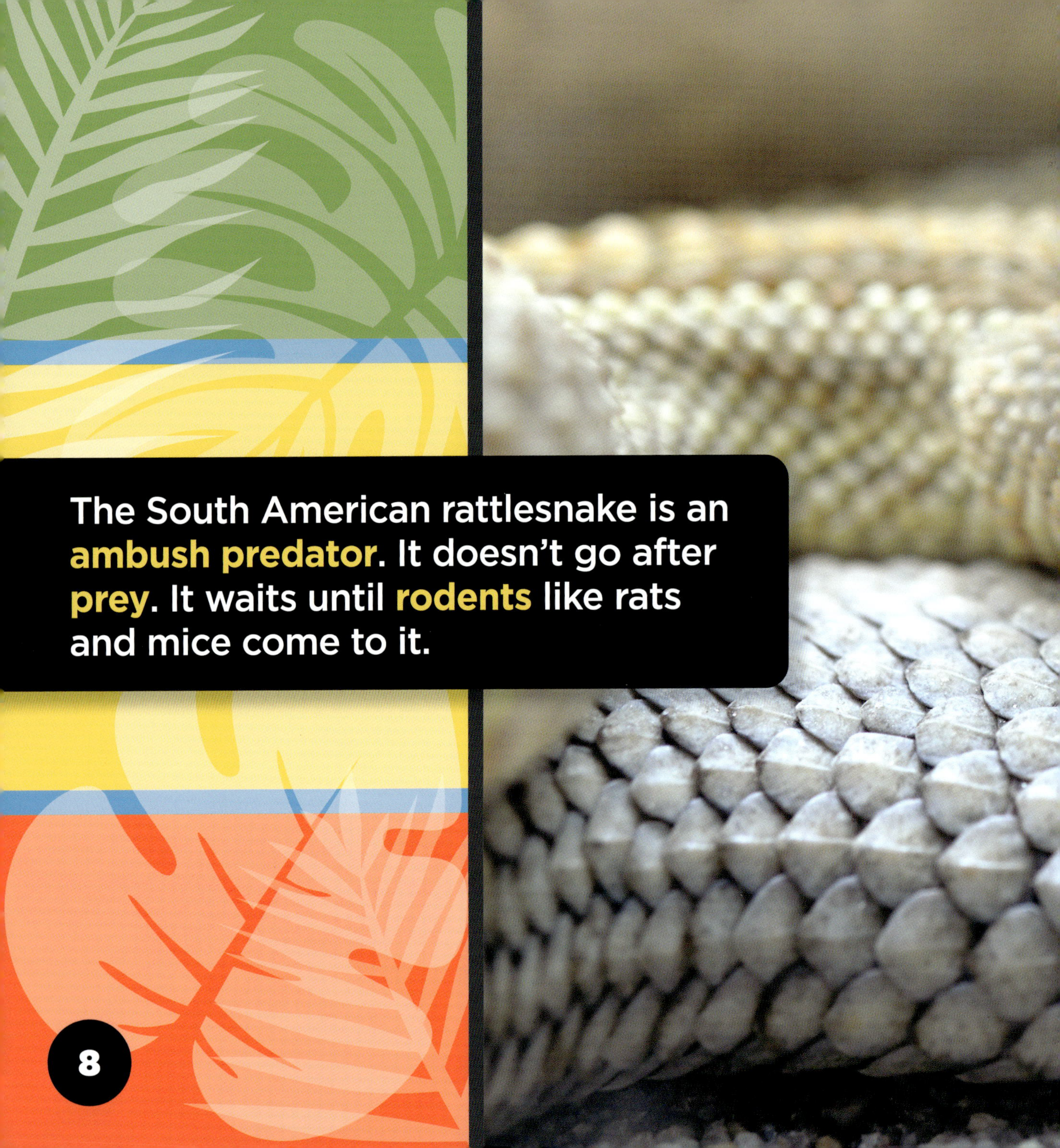

The South American rattlesnake is an **ambush predator**. It doesn't go after **prey**. It waits until **rodents** like rats and mice come to it.

The rattlesnake is dark brown or light green with a diamond-shaped pattern on its skin. The color helps them disappear in the desert and other dry **habitats**. They use their **camouflage** to hide from predators and to stay low-key when trying to capture their prey.

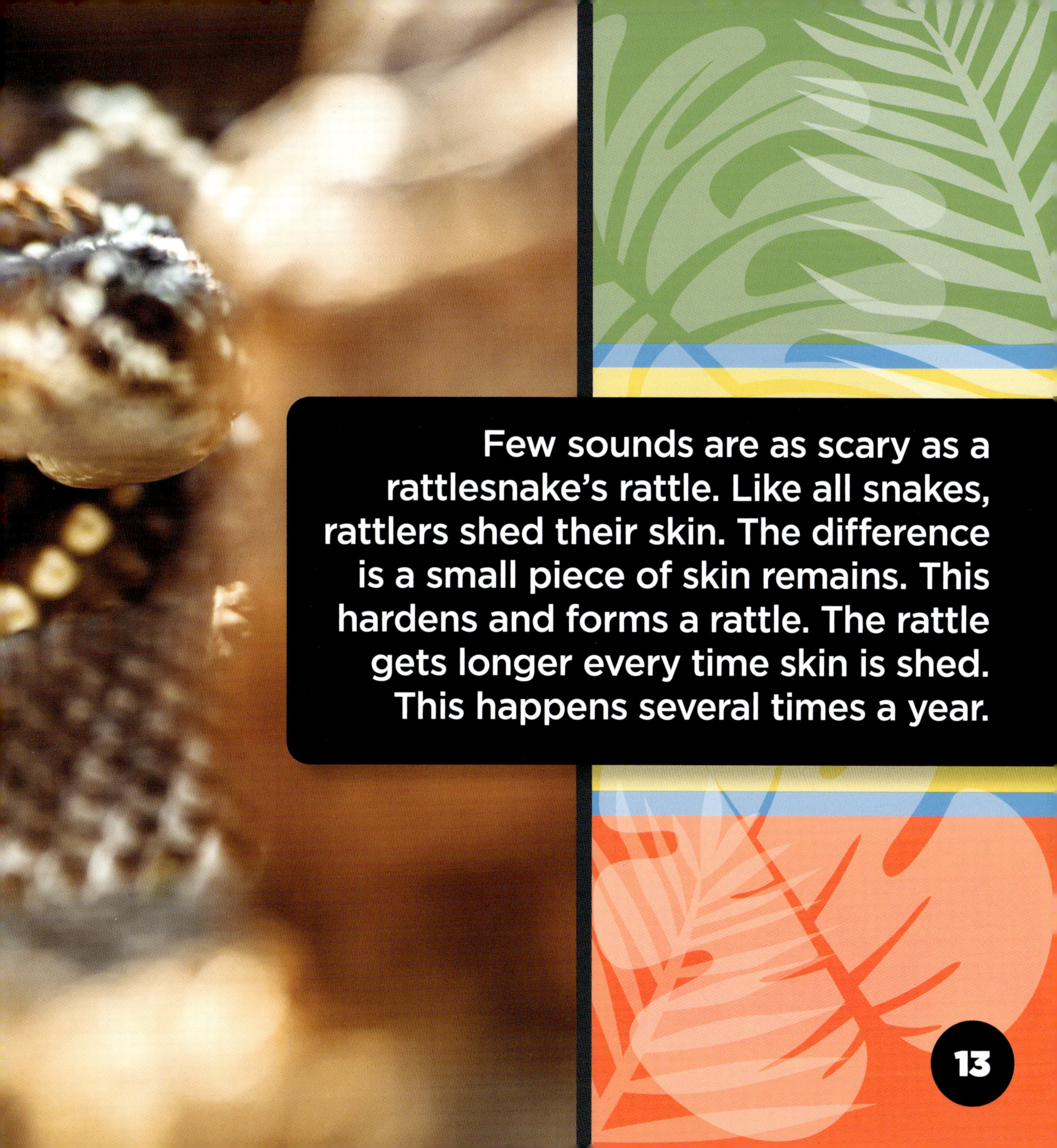

Few sounds are as scary as a rattlesnake's rattle. Like all snakes, rattlers shed their skin. The difference is a small piece of skin remains. This hardens and forms a rattle. The rattle gets longer every time skin is shed. This happens several times a year.

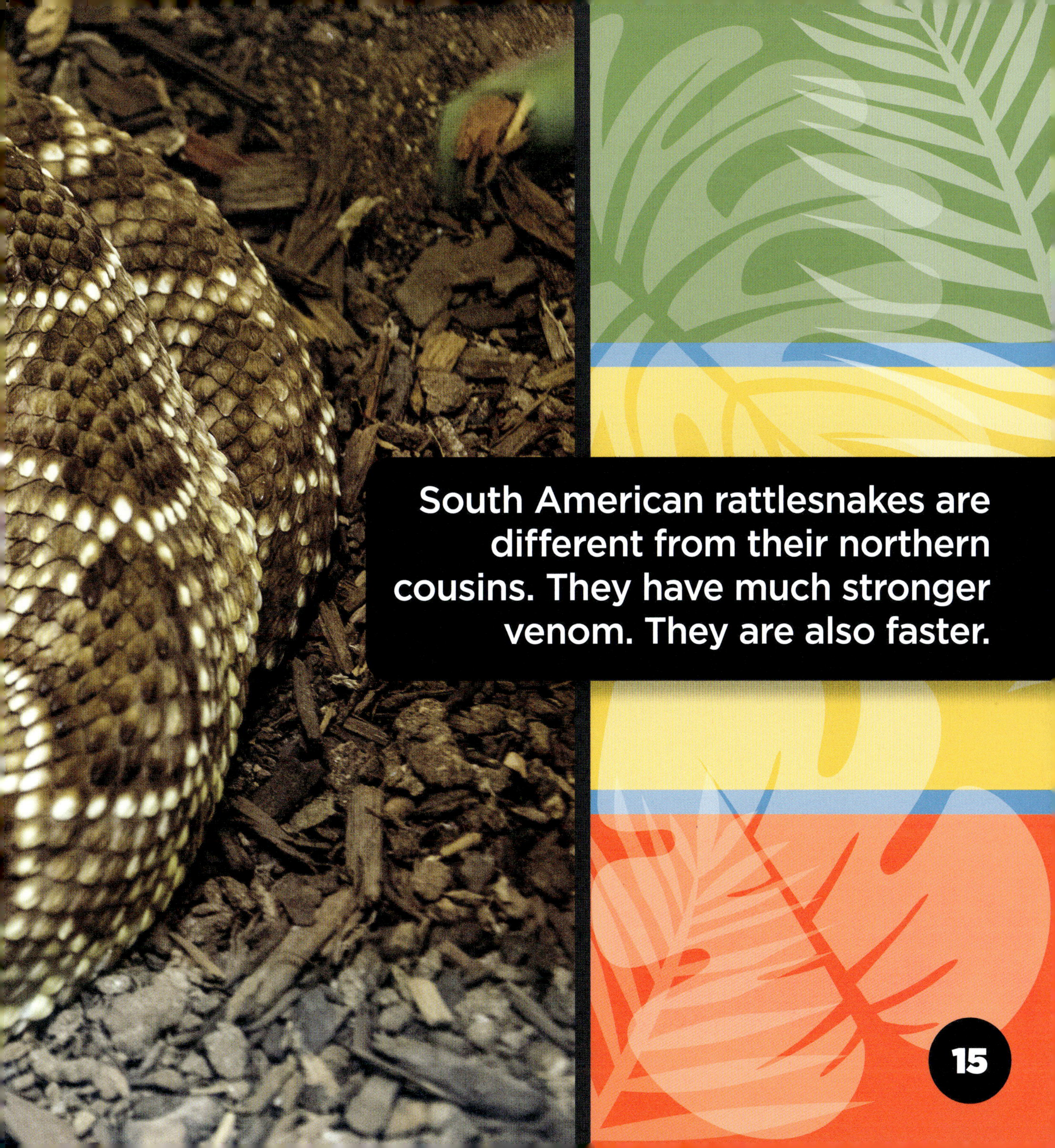

South American rattlesnakes are different from their northern cousins. They have much stronger venom. They are also faster.

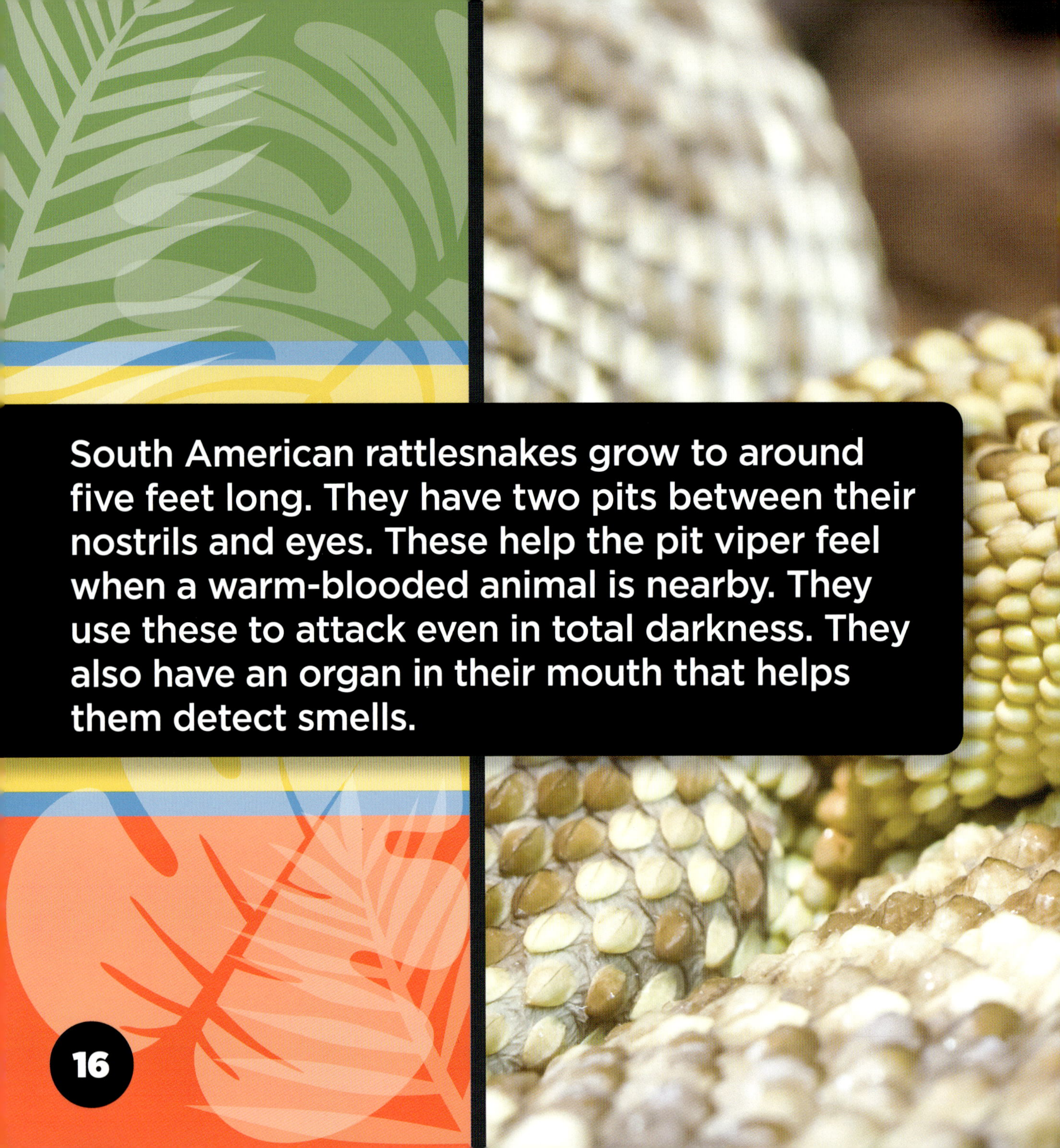

South American rattlesnakes grow to around five feet long. They have two pits between their nostrils and eyes. These help the pit viper feel when a warm-blooded animal is nearby. They use these to attack even in total darkness. They also have an organ in their mouth that helps them detect smells.

Like other pit vipers, the rattlesnake gives birth to live young. Usually around six are born at a time. The babies are also deadly. Their venom is stronger than an adult's.

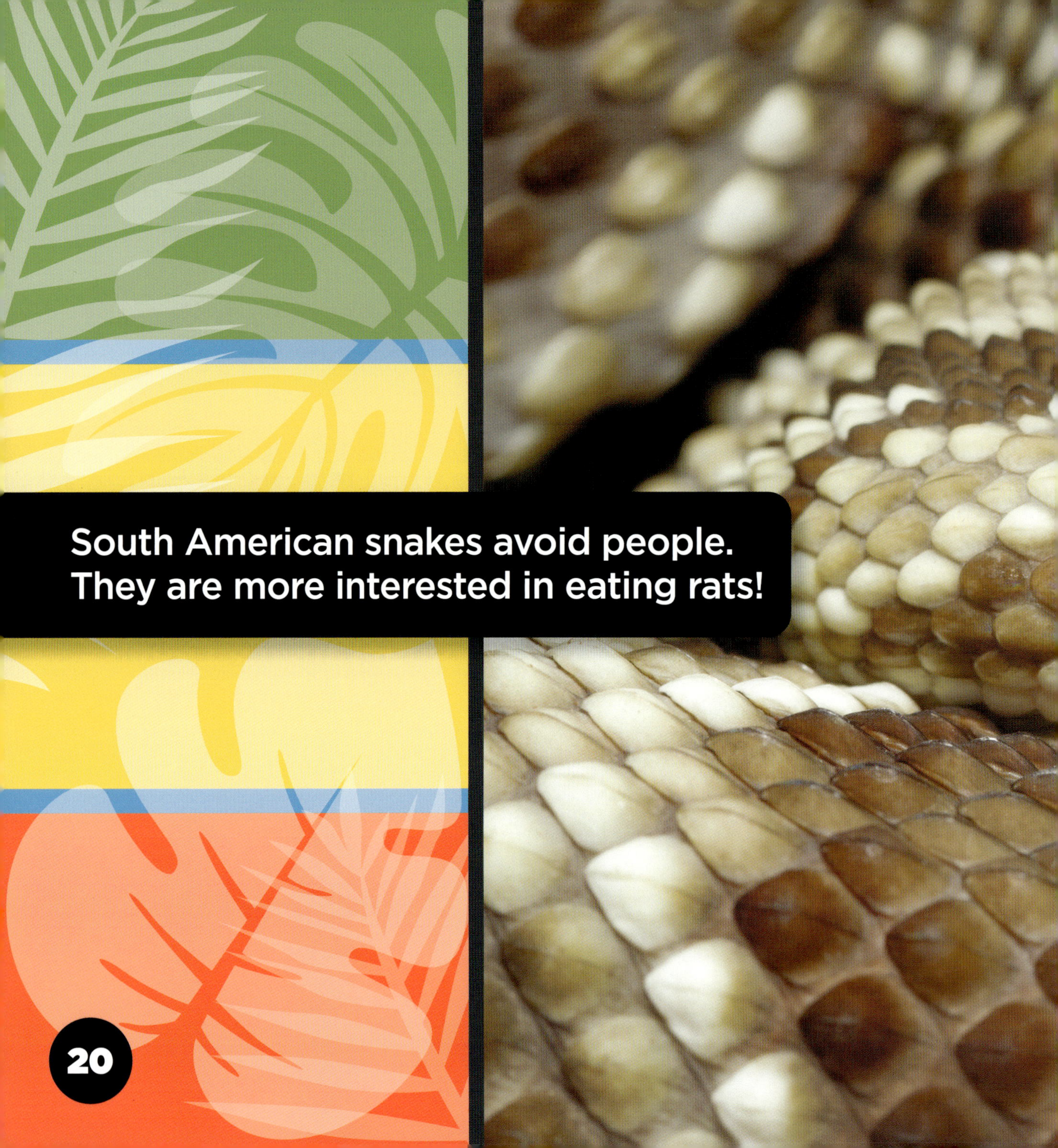

South American snakes avoid people.
They are more interested in eating rats!

Where Do South American Rattlesnakes Live?

They live across the northern parts of South America, including the countries of Argentina, Bolivia, Brazil, Columbia, French Guiana, Peru, and Venezuela.

Interesting Facts

- Native tribes once used South American rattlesnake venom on arrows.
- The South American rattlesnake only needs to eat once every two weeks.
- Its venom can cause blindness.
- The kingsnake, a main rattlesnake predator, is unaffected by its venom.
- The rattlesnake is considered a very new snake. It hasn't been on this planet as long as other snakes.

Parts of a South American Rattlesnake

Head

The rattlesnake's hollow fangs can be over four inches long. They fold into the snake's mouth. It has two pits between nostrils and eyes that sense heat. It also has an organ in its mouth it uses to smell.

Eyes

Its eyes work very well at night, although it can find prey using its pits. It is very good at noticing movement but doesn't see as clearly as a human.

Body

The skin is normally folded and stretches out during a meal.

Glossary

ambush predator
A meat-eating animal that captures its target secretly rather than by speed or strength

camouflage
Colors that let animals blend into their surroundings

fangs
The teeth of a venomous snake by which poison is injected

habitat
The natural home of an animal

prey
Animal hunted by another for food

rodents
An animal whose teeth keep growing like a mouse or a rat

venom
Poison used by an animal

Further Reading

Dunn, Mary. *Rattlesnakes*. North Mankato, Minn.: Capstone Press. 2014.

Gregory, Josh. *Rattlesnakes*. NY: Scholastic. 2015.

Hirschmann, Kris. *Top Ten Deadly Snakes: Go Face to Fang with the World's 10 Deadliest Snakes*. 2020.

Kim, Carol. *Pit Viper (World's Coolest Snakes)*. Vero Beach, FL: Rourke. 2018.

Starkey, Michael G. *Snakes for Kids: A Junior Scientist's Guide to Venom, Scales, and Life in the Wild*. Emeryville, CA: Rockridge Press. 2020.

On the Internet

Find out more about the South American rattlesnake from Kidadl:
https://kidadl.com/facts/animals/south-american-rattlesnake-facts

The San Diego Zoo has info on all types of rattlesnakes:
https://animals.sandiegozoo.org/animals/rattlesnake

This video shows a South American rattlesnake slithering in its natural habitat:
https://www.youtube.com/watch?v=5L4bjVS1AhQ

Index